# THE
# COLLISION
## *Vol. 1*

## 20 Thought-Provoking Articles on Christ and Culture

## Daniel Blackaby

Blackaby Ministries International
Jonesboro, Georgia

# The Collision

*Equipping Christians to navigate today's digital, media-driven culture by strengthening their biblical foundations, addressing difficult questions about their faith, and guiding them to engage thoughtfully with today's pop culture and secular worldviews.*

THE COLLISION VOLUME ONE: 20 THOUGHT PROVOKING
ARTICLES ON CHRIST AND CULTURE
PUBLISHED BY BLACKABY MINISTRIES INTERNATIONAL
P.O Box 1035
Jonesboro, GA 30237

ISBN 978-1-7338536-6-8

Printed in the United States of America
2020 - 1st ed

# Contents

# INTRODUCTION

Countless cultural conversations are happening all around you. Are you aware of them? More importantly, are you actively engaged and contributing to them? In today's media-saturated, increasingly digital world, these cultural conversations are right at your fingertips. They're also at everybody else's fingertips, and—one way or another—they constitute the world in which we live.

Reality has always both reflected and been shaped by the movies we watch, the music we listen to, and the books we read. What starts as imaginative technology in a science fiction film becomes reality a few decades later. If you want to know what the world will look like tomorrow, look at pop culture today. By the same token, if you want to know what ideologies and worldviews will reign tomorrow, just look at what ideologies and worldviews pop culture is preaching and normalizing today.

Pop culture is the arena in which many of the crucial conversations about faith, morality, and truth are taking place. The Church can ill-afford to remain aloof or passive. Now, more than ever, Christians need

1

to listen to these conversations and let their voices be heard. When we do, a collision between Christ and culture is inevitable.

The only question is . . . *are you ready for the collision*?

## About the Collision

Several years ago, my brother Mike and I published a book called *When Worlds Collide: Stepping Up and Standing Out in an Anti-God Culture* (B&H Books). The simple message of that book is that life is filled with spiritual collisions, and how we respond to them has far-reaching consequences for us and the world around us. We can respond in one of three ways:

1) We **Cave-In** by compromising our Christian values to blend into the unbelieving world around us.
2) We become a **Cave-Dweller** and attempt to hide behind the safety of the church walls, avoiding collisions all together.
3) We become a **Collider** by impacting the world for Christ head on.

The book's message resonated with a lot of people. Many readers expressed a desire to become a Collider. But, inevitably, some questions quickly followed: what next? What does being a Collider look like? How should I collide with _____ or _____? **The Collision** provides an answer to those questions.

The Collision was launched in March 2019 as a division of Blackaby Ministries International. I started The Collision as a digital, multi-media platform aimed at equipping Christians to navigate the inevitable collisions between Christ and culture. By leveraging online articles, YouTube videos, books, and social media, we've sought to cultivate honest cultural conversations about the important issues Christians face today and to encourage Christians to collide with the world for Christ.

## About This Book

This book is a snapshot of a year full of spiritual collisions and cultural conversations. The 15 articles and five pop culture reviews included in this book first appeared on our website (**thecollision. org**). Each of these articles was posted in 2019 and, as a result, some of the details are topical to specific moments or events in time. As a little green puppet named Yoda once mused, "Always in motion is the future." As the pop culture train chugs full steam down the tracks, some of the specifics of these articles may become recontextualized in light of newer developments. Keep that in mind as you read this book.

At the same time, fix your eyes on the forest, not the trees. Cultural engagement as a Christian is not a one-off action. It is a daily commission. These articles will not provide all the answers—although I pray you find answers within these pages. Rather, this book exists to demonstrate a mindset, approach, and general posture. In other words, this book is not just about collisions—it's about *colliders* and what it looks like to become one.

## Become a Collider

As you may have noticed, this book is *volume one*. We will publish volume *two* next year, and, hopefully, volume *three* the year after that. If you enjoy this first collection, I hope you will consider checking out each new annual anthology. More importantly, I hope you will join our community of Christians from all around the world as together we seek to collide with the world for Christ. Join the movement by connecting with us:

**Website:** thecollision.org
**YouTube:** Youtube.com/c/thecollisionbmi
**Facebook:** @Thecollisionbmi
**Twitter:** @Thecollisionbmi

# Part One

# POP CULTURE
# COLLISIONS

# 1

# Engaging Culture as Irrelevant Christians

In today's culture, Christians are labelled an assortment of four-letter words (most of which cannot be printed in this Christian book!). The word "cool" is rarely among these descriptors. The world largely views the Church as out of touch and old fashioned.

Some Christians treat their irrelevance as a badge of honor. They may not live in a secluded mountaintop monastery, but they remain figuratively isolated from the culture around them.

They feel pride as they use social media to declare their disengagement from culture: "I STILL haven't seen a single Star Wars movie! Who's with me?" And if they skip the next Avengers film, their Facebook timeline will undoubtedly let you know.

## "Relevant" Christians

Not all Christians are satisfied with this isolationist approach. Christians often declare the need to be "relevant" for the sake of the Gospel. In practice, this desire often leads the Church to transport pop culture inside its walls in hopes of leading people into the sanctuary.

The world loves Marvel superhero movies? Let's do a sermon series emphasizing how Jesus demonstrates the best characteristics of all the Avengers: "Our God is powerful like the Hulk! Virtuous like Captain America! Divine like Thor!"

> **Christians don't need to inject pop culture into the Church to have a relevant message. The Gospel is relevant.**

*Game of Thrones* is popular? "Today's sermon is about how you can allow God to win the game of thrones in *your* life and reign on the iron throne of your heart!"

When the hit series *Lost* ruled the TV landscape, preachers had a heyday with the low-hanging fruit it provided: "We're all *Lost* on a spiritual island without Jesus. Can I get an amen?"

## The Relevancy of the Gospel

Despite the person's good intentions, this approach is superficial. Pop culture becomes little more than a vibrant coat of paint sloshed over the Church's seemingly pallid message. Christians try to convince the world that they're relevant by "name dropping" popular movies. But their insincere method has the opposite effect.

Christians don't need to inject pop culture into the Church to have a relevant message. The Gospel *is* relevant. Humanity is as sinful, fallen, and in need of a savior as we've ever been, and the Gospel provides an answer that is as powerful as it has always been. The manifestations of culture are constantly in flux, but the Gospel of Christ is timeless.

## Culturally Engaged Christians

There is a significant difference between being culturally **relevant** and being culturally **engaged**. A longing for acceptance drives the former, whereas the urgency of the Gospel fuels the latter.

I've heard many Christians justify watching a mind-numbing amount of television because it keeps them "up to date" with the culture. To reach lost people, they say, we need to speak their language. This statement contains a kernel of truth. Pop culture has always been a communal, bridge-building phenomenon that provides common ground Christians can leverage for divine purposes.

At the same time, Christians don't need to catch every obscure *Friends* or *Breaking Bad* reference to relate to the culture. Christians aren't increasing their witness simply by *consuming* pop culture ("Yeah, baby! I'm watching Netflix for Jesus this weekend!"). Christians need to go beyond trivia or consumption and *engage* with culture.

Rather than hijacking pop culture trends to spruce up our message, Christians should take our message to pop culture. We *should* keep our fingers on the pulse of pop culture, not to impress the world with our trivia but because many of the crucial moral, spiritual, and worldview issues are being reflected *in* and influenced *by* the entertainment industry. Pop culture has always been a preview of coming attractions. If you want to know what the world will be like tomorrow, look at pop culture today.

Christians must join the cultural conversation. Not to be "cool" or accepted but because we have something important to contribute to the discussion.

Pop culture doesn't have anything to contribute to the Gospel, but the Gospel has everything to contribute to pop culture. Important discussions are happening, worldviews are being shaped, and Christians should be right in the thick of it.

> "Christians must join the cultural conversation. Not to be "cool" or accepted but because we have something important to contribute to the discussion."

It's not wrong or sinful if you are an undefeated juggernaut at Star Wars trivial pursuit (as I happen to be) or can spout off an endless supply of *The Office* quotes or classic rock song lyrics. Just remember that we have much more to offer the world than superficial information. Christianity is not always "trendy" or "cool," but its message will always be relevant.

# 2

# "Can Christians Watch R-Rated Movies?": A Christian Approach to Making Wise Entertainment Choices

*"Is it okay for Christians to watch R-Rated movies?"*
*"Oh, I don't think I can watch that. Isn't it rated R?"*
*"This looks interesting, but what's it rated?*

Christians frequently ask these questions. In a broader sense, the unifying concern is about which entertainment choices are permissible for Christians. This important question deserves a thoughtful answer.

Visual art has simplistic categorization: pornographic and not pornographic. Ditto for music (explicit or not explicit). Books are the Wild West with no "official" rating system. Of all the entertainment mediums, movies are the exception. You are probably familiar with the MPAA (Motion Picture Association of America) rating system of G, PG, PG-13, R, and NC-17.

Which of these ratings indicate the movie is permissible for Christians to watch? My grandfather often says that if you ask the wrong questions, you will get the wrong answers.

Relying on a rigid rating system does not actually protect us from danger, and it robs us of experiencing the full joy and power cinema offers. The following are three guidelines for how Christians should approach film and entertainment choices.

## 1. We Must Reject a Posture of Fear

Implicit in the questions Christians ask about movies is *fear.* Christians tend to approach a film with the question, "Will this be harmful?" rather than "Can this be beneficial?" Within the Church is a lingering stigma that the film industry is nothing but a dangerous cesspool of sin and sacrilege. Though this belief is somewhat warranted, it doesn't tell the *full* story.

> **We were not created to live recklessly, but neither should we live in fear.**

Imagine going to a beach and staying in the shade one hundred feet away from the water for fear of sunburns or drowning. Both are real dangers, and we would be foolish to neglect sunscreen or do away with lifeguards. But it would be tragic to allow these fears to steal the joy of our beach vacation. We were not created to live recklessly, but neither should we live in fear.

God loves stories so much that when He inspired the Bible—His perfect and timeless self-revelation—He primarily used stories (more than 60% of the Bible is written in narrative form). When Jesus came to Earth as a man, He spent much of His earthly ministry telling stories ("he said nothing to them without a parable." Matt 13:34). Stories have the power to communicate important truth and transform us, not just to corrupt or distract us.

## 2. We Must Go Beyond the Surface

Many Christians base their assessment of films entirely on the presence or absence of "bad stuff," by which they generally mean the Big Three: violence, sex, and profanity. They ask, "What's the language like?" "Is there much violence?" "Is there any nudity?" Again, these are important questions—but they shouldn't be our only questions.

One issue with establishing a standard based solely on a particular content-based rating—such as R—is that it suggests that anything with a lower rating is harmless or permissible. If you've read any of the movie reviews at The Collision, you know that our format examines content that is both "on the surface" (violence/sex/profanity) and "beneath the surface" (worldview/messages). When Christians focus only on the former, they inadvertently neglect the latter, and the result can be disastrous. In fact, what is beneath the surface can be more perilous than what is immediately evident.

Christians can potentially (though not always) benefit from watching a thought-provoking and powerful film that contains one needlessly gratuitous sex scene if they simply skip the graphic scene (like cutting the bruised portion off an otherwise tasty banana). On the other hand, a distorted and secular worldview that underpins an entire story is so subversive that it contaminates the whole film. Take *Smallfoot* (2018), a squeaky-clean PG children's film that has a relentless and militant atheistic worldview latent throughout. The MPAA rating system might focus only on the surface-level content, but Christians can ill-afford to do the same.

## 3. We Must Recognize That Not All "Bad" Content is Actually Bad.

Not all R-Rated content is created equal. In fact, the most successful R-Rated movie in cinematic history is Mel Gibson's *The Passion of the Christ*. The Bible itself certainly warrants a hard R rating; it is stuffed with enough violence, sex, rape, vulgarity, murder, and incest to make the creative executives at HBO blush. The R-rated content in the Bible suggests that there is a time, place, and manner in which Christians not only *can* confront and engage with such material but *should*.

Many of the most powerful war films are understandably rated R. To water down or sugarcoat the grim reality of war would be untruthful and dubious. Similarly, a movie like Steven Spielberg's *Schindler's List* contains plenty of violence, nudity, and profanity, but no one is likely to feel enthralled or sexually aroused by watching it. Rather, the graphic nature of the film enables the viewer to understand the horrors of the Holocaust in ways that a paragraph in a history textbook never will.

Of course, sometimes "bad" content is just that—*bad*. The popular *SAW* franchise contains gruesome violence as well, but unlike a sobering war film, the horror films glorify violence rather than exposing it as ugly. A gristly prison film may contain strong profanity as it paints a dismaying picture of our true broken and sinful human nature, while a raunchy stoner comedy tosses out F-Bombs like they're lollipops at a 4th of July parade just for juvenile kicks.

## So...What's the Answer Then?

The point is not that Christians shouldn't be discerning or cautious with their entertainment choices. If anything, the point is that they should be *more* discerning and cautious. A blanket rule like "Christians cannot watch R-Rated films" is far too generalized and simplistic for something as complex and nuanced as a film. So how should we choose what films to watch and where to draw the line? Here are three quick guidelines:

*Do Your Homework.* Go beyond the rating. If a film interests you, do some research. There are plenty of helpful resources on the internet, such as the weekly movie reviews we do at TheCollision.org.

> There is far more danger in judging or questioning other Christians' eternal salvation on the basis of the movies they watch than in anything harmful in the movies themselves.

*Develop Accountability.* Don't let the entertainment industry have power over you. If your initial research reveals that a film includes a gratuitous sex scene, for example, hold off on seeing it in theaters. Wait until it comes out on home video or streaming and watch it with

15

your remote control nearby to skip the scene. Better yet, watch it with a group of friends or family to ensure you *do* skip the scene or quit watching the film altogether if you discern partway through that you should.

***Recognize that there is room for liberty.*** The Bible does not provide a clear step-by-step guide for how to consume entertainment, but it *does* tell us how to honor God and respect one another. Not everyone will approach entertainment in the same way. There is far more danger in judging or questioning other Christians' eternal salvation on the basis of the movies they watch than in anything harmful in the movies themselves.

# 3

# "Spoilers!" and Our Deep Yearning for a Satisfying Experience

The internet has—for better or worse—changed society in significant ways. One of these ways is our experience of art and entertainment. Social media has given increased power to the dreaded S-Word—*spoilers*.

*Spoilers* is a buzzword today. It refers to revealing important plot details from a movie or book in advance. It is not uncommon for passionate fans to "go dark" for weeks—even *months*—before an upcoming movie by removing themselves from all social media. Other people wear headphones into the movie theater to block out any chatter from those leaving the film. When plot details about a movie leak to the public before its release (as happened with *Avengers: Endgame*), society goes into a full-blown panic.

In order to understand our culture's obsession with spoilers, we must understand what it is that is being spoiled. So, consider how much

17

society has changed. Try to guess which movie the following quote describes:

*"The emperor's secret weapon is destroyed, the princess is rescued, and the forces of evil routed in a final spaceship dogfight conducted along World War II lines. The sinister Black Knight is allowed to slink away, however, to scheme again another day, thereby keeping the door open for possible sequel."*[1]

As you likely guessed, the quote is from George Lucas describing the climatic third act of *Star Wars* beat by beat. The interview was published in *The New York Times* on September 12, 1976. The film itself debuted in theaters on May 25th...of 1977!

Yes, the director was unreservedly spoiling the end of the movie a year before it was even released to the public. These days, not even the *title* of a Star Wars film is revealed until 6-7 months before the release date, let alone any significant story beats. What changed?

For starters, there was no such thing as home video. VHS tapes were not introduced into American culture until August 1977. If you wanted to see a movie, you'd better see it in theaters. The fanatics who famously lined up around the block to see *Star Wars* in theaters didn't know if they would ever have the chance to see it again. Knowing the plot ahead of time was irrelevant, because simply going to the theater itself was a special experience. In an age when a movie can be streamed on an iPhone less than 3 months after it hits theaters, this cultural rite has been lost.

Cinema's power has never wholly been in the stories themselves; it's in the *experience*. People don't just want to see a movie. They want the *experience* of seeing a movie. Fear of spoilers is our culture's last-ditch effort to preserve the cinematic experience. The movie theater industry is aware of this desperation. Rather than reduce prices, theater chains have done the opposite. They've rolled out pricier food options and more comfortable seating. Theaters understand that they are not so much in the movie industry as they are in the *experience* industry.

In recent years, big name directors such as Steven Spielberg and Christopher Nolan have crusaded against the movie streaming industry (Netflix, Hulu, Amazon Prime, etc.). Television shows like *Game of Thrones* are popular, in part, because they are the last of a dying breed of "event TV" (as was *Lost*). Hollywood is proving the old adage true that you can indeed have too much of a good thing. In an age when cinematic storytelling is more pervasive and easier to access than ever before, there is a growing sense that the coveted cinematic experience itself is slipping away and leaving a great void.

> " What keeps many young people from a vibrant faith is not an issue with Christianity's message, but a disconnect from the experience of faith.

## What Does this Mean for the Church?

This deep yearning for an experience is a double-edged sword. On the one hand, how can the Church operate in a world that values the *experience* of content more than the content itself? Many people today expect to be entertained. They leave a church service saying,

"Man, I just didn't get anything out of the service today," as though they had just witnessed a disappointing Broadway performance rather than entering into the presence of the almighty God of the universe.

On the other hand, people are clearly yearning for a genuine and satisfying experience. They aren't interested in merely hearing information and facts. They want it to impact their daily life. In fact, according to the most recent statistics, the majority of those who leave the Church today are not motivated by doctrinal issues. They are leaving because they sense a disconnect between their "church life" and what they experience Monday through Saturday. In other words, what keeps many young people from a vibrant faith is not an issue with Christianity's message, but a disconnect from the experience of faith.

As the psalmist wrote, "Taste and see that the Lord is good" (Psalms 34:8). The Christian faith was never supposed to be merely an intellectual or knowledge-based ideology. It was intended to be an experience of abundant life.

Every year—from Comic-Con to Dragon-Con to Star Wars Celebration—thousands of people join together in sweaty convention centers in search of a satisfying communal experience. Fandoms have become a quasi-religious

> **The Christian faith can offer something far beyond and infinitely more satisfying than any cinematic experience or fandom, and no amount of internet leaks can spoil it.**

movement, with their own sacred texts, holy sites, and rituals. People want to feel connected to an experience that is bigger than themselves.

20

This widespread desire is good news, for the Christian faith can offer something far beyond and infinitely more satisfying than any cinematic experience or fandom, and no amount of internet leaks can spoil it.

# 4

# Hollywood: America's New Religion

America is in a religious decline. At least, that's what we're constantly being told. Despite these declarations, statistically speaking, America remains predominantly religious with only a small (albeit growing) population of professed atheists. As any anthropological study reveals, religious worship is a human default. No civilization ever started out as atheists.

That America is becoming more hostile to biblical Christianity does not indicate that it is becoming less religious. People are merely embracing new religions. One such religion is the god of science, driven forward by Darwin's gospel, a naturalistic worldview, and the great commission to proselytize the doctrines of secular humanism.

But there is another rapidly growing, yet rarely considered religion— the religion of Hollywood.

# The Holy Church of Hollywood

A "religion" is defined as "a cause, principle, or system of beliefs held with ardor and faith" that offers an overarching narrative and ideal for people to strive toward. In this regard, Hollywood certainly fits the bill. The cinematic experience has always been ripe with religious overtones.

Writing about Louis B. Mayer—the founder of MGM Studios and a patriarch of the Hollywood faith—one biographer concludes that his achievement was to "provide a reassurance against the anxieties and disruptions of the time. He did so by fashioning a vast, compelling national fantasy out of his dreams and out of the basic tenets of his own dogmatic faith."[2] These founding sentiments continue to this day.

First, you have the **temples**. Despite the doom-and-gloom prophecies about the impact of the home streaming industry, the movie theater remains a staple in American society (2019 surpassed 2018 as the highest grossing year in history). Much like the Christian church under Emperor Constantine's reign, these cinematic temples are growing increasingly extravagant and ornate. As you enter the hallowed temple doors, you are usually met with a high ceiling, the iconography of movie posters lining the walls, and the alluring incense of the concession stand.

Next comes the **worship service**. At the appointed hour, congregants make their way from the fellowship time in the lobby to the auditorium to take their seats. The service begins with announcements (of course), as listeners learn about future events and happenings. Then the lights dim, and for the next two hours the attendees listen attentively to the well-crafted and refined message.

No religion is complete without **prophets**. Actors—whose job consists of convincing viewers to accept a lie—proclaim social and moral guidance and truth. A woman who portrays an angsty teenager in a raunchy rom-com stands alongside US presidents and presidential candidates, and men who spent a decade donning skin-tight superhero spandex are suddenly the prophetic authority on issues such as racism, political policy, and climate change.

For the especially devout, there are opportunities for a holy **pilgrimage** to cinematic Mecca. Every year, thousands of zealous fans flood convention centers for Comic-Con and other pop culture celebrations. Of course, most religions experience some in-fighting, and within the cinematic religion are various diverging **denominations**. Bitter feuds, such as the clash between Marvel and DC fandoms or the Disney Star Wars vs. Pre-Disney Star Wars crowds, have reduced countless internet comment sections and social media news feeds to a toxic sludge of negativity and anger.

Perhaps most important, however, is that the cinematic religion is propelled by **devotion.** Consider the ultimately successful campaign to re-release *Avengers: Endgame* just a month after it left theaters so it could surpass *Avatar* as the #1 box-office grossing movie of all time (although this "victory" ignores inflation and swelling ticket prices, but I digress). Fans, many of whom had already dished out $13 to see the movie, dutifully bought tickets several more times in order to help support the mission—even though both films are properties of Disney, whose executives were undoubtedly dancing all the way to their Scrooge McDuck-esque bank vaults.

# No God but God

This article is not an anti-Hollywood rant. You can be a faithful Christian and a passionate cinephile at the same time. You can eagerly anticipate the next comic book film or wear a Pikachu onesie to a geek convention without compromising your Christian faith.

The problem is when we allow pop culture to fill a larger role than it should and become more religiously devout toward cinema and fandoms than to God and His Church. No one is likely to claim "Hollywood " as their official religion on the next census, but actions reveal were religious loyalty truly lies.

Some people can't stop talking about the latest blockbuster movie they saw but rarely (if ever) share about God's activity in their life. They spend ungodly amounts of time down the rabbit hole of fan theories and speculation but never mature beyond a shallow, surface-level interpretation of scripture. They dish out money at the theater kiosk to help a mega corporation like *Disney* win an unofficial competition against itself but fail to tithe to their local church to help win souls for Christ.

> The problem is when we allow pop culture to fill a larger role than it should and become more religiously devout toward cinema and fandoms than to God and His Church.

Pop culture and cinema can be beautiful, but they make horrible gods. Part of what makes movies so engrossing and captivating is also what makes their danger so seductive and powerful. If we long to impact our culture for Christ, we must be wary of how large a foothold we allow pop culture to occupy. Movies and fandoms provide immense delight, community, and excitement, but true abundant life and salvation are found in Christ alone. Let's make sure the way we talk, spend our time, and arrange our priorities reflects this truth.

# 5

# Do Violent Movies Make Us Violent People?

Art impacts us. This claim is indisputable, having been backed by a breadth of scientific data and centuries of work in aesthetic philosophy. The more important—and far more difficult—questions are **how much** and **in what way?**

These questions resurfaced in the wake of the horrific Parkland school shooting, when President Trump announced that he would meet with representatives from the video game industry to discuss the relationship between *virtual* violence and *real-world* violence. Similar concerns sparked by the 2017 Las Vegas shooting led Netflix to delay the release of their violent action series *The Punisher*.

This is the important question: *Do violent movies and video games cause us to become violent people?*

The answer is not as simple as we might assume.

# Two Different Perspectives

The debate is actually an ancient one, pre-dating the film industry by many centuries. In a simplified form, the discussion traces back to the opposing philosophies of the great Greek thinkers Plato and Aristotle.

For **Plato**, the theater (the precursor to the modern cinema) enflamed man's passions and inspired imitation. In *Republic,* he writes that art "feeds and waters down passions instead of drying them up; she lets them rule, although they ought to be controlled."[3] In contemporary terms, the person who watches a *Fast and Furious* movie filled with high-throttle car chases is likely to leave the theater and go drive fast and furiously.

Echoes of this sentiment emerged with the 2012 shooting in Colorado. The tragedy occurred in a movie theater during a showing of the Batman film *The Dark Knight Rises*. The shooter's apartment was later found decorated with Batman paraphernalia, and his brightly dyed hair evoked quick comparisons to The Joker (Batman's arch-nemesis). Perhaps most unsettling is that a preview for the crime-drama *Gangster Squad* had been playing before the film in many theaters (although not in Colorado) with a scene portraying criminals unleashing machine gun fire into a movie theater. The trailer was quickly pulled from circulation, the movie was delayed, and re-shoots were conducted to change the location of that scene, but the eerie similarities left a lasting cultural impression.

**Aristotle**, on the other hand, offered a more optimistic perspective. Rather than enflaming the passions, art offered a form of *catharsis*, which purged negative passions and desires. In this way, art is akin to a fluffy pillow that an angry child beats his fist against in place of his brother's face or how a father wrestles with his boys so their natural aggression can be expressed in a controlled manner.

> **Humans are complex. Art is complex. It is no surprise that the human experience of art is equally complex.**

In short, Plato would argue that a violent action movie instills similar violence in the viewers, whereas Aristotle would claim that a violent movie quenches the violence that *already exists within* us and allows us to "get it out of our system." The modern debate has largely followed in this same duality.

So, who is right? The answer is *they both are.*

Humans are complex. Art is complex. It is no surprise that the human experience of art is equally complex. While today's society is often defined by emotional knee-jerk reactions and a rush toward extremes, this issue warrants a more nuanced and thoughtful discussion.

For example, was the Colorado shooter enflamed with vicious passion and driven to commit horrible violence because he watched a Batman movie? *Impossible to know.* What *is* clear is that a one-to-one correlation is dubious. Keep in mind that more than **50 million** people watched *The Dark Knight Rises* in theaters. If the film inspired violence, it seemingly did so in only **0.000002%** of the audience. Patrick Markey, psychology professor at Villanova University, offers the example of watching a sad movie.[4] While the audience will likely leave the theater in a more somber mood, few would claim that the experience inevitably results in long-term clinical depression.

## How Then Should Christians Deal with Violence in Art?

With much thought, prayer, and discernment. Violence in art takes many forms that should not all be lumped into a single condemnation of "movie violence" or "video game violence." The danger of violence depicted in art is not with violence itself, but with certain gratuitous expressions of violence. Consider the following:

*"Ehud reached with his left hand, drew the sword from his right thigh and plunged it into the king's belly. Even the handle sank in after the blade, and his bowels discharged. Ehud did not pull the sword out, and the fat closed in over it."*

No, this scene is not from *Game of Thrones.* It comes from inspired scripture (Judges 3:21-22)! The Old Testament is *brimming* with violence. Why all the grisly details? Perhaps because violence is a reality of our world. If art and storytelling are to delve deeply and honestly into the human experience, violence must be explored.

In defense of violence in fantasy stories, C.S. Lewis wrote,

"Let there be wicked kings and beheadings, battles and dungeons, giants and dragons, and let villains be soundly killed at the end of the book [...] It would be nice if no little boy in bed, hearing, or thinking he hears, a sound, were ever at all frightened. But if he is going to be frightened, I think it better that he should think of giants and dragons than merely of burglars. And I think St George, or any bright champion in armor, is a better comfort than the idea of the police."[5]

His point is that adults cannot shelter themselves or their children from violence. Art should explore these themes in a manner that is *honest to* but still *separate from* reality. The question, then, is not ***should we*** explore violence in art, but ***how should we*** do it.

## Final Food For Thought

Does violent art make us violent people? Not necessarily.

Should we protest against movie violence? It depends on the type of movie violence.

Should Christians watch violent movies? It depends on the movie and on the person.

The point is not to give a clear-cut answer.

The point is that there ***isn't*** a clear-cut answer.

Broad rules like *Christians shouldn't watch R-Rated movies* miss the mark. Art influences us, but the influence is not always *negative*. Violence will always—and *should* always—have a place in art. Clearly, discernment is required when determining where to draw the line, but judgement calls are necessary in every area of the Christian life, not just regarding movies.

> **The violence we experience in art might be shocking or even appalling—but perhaps that's not always such a bad thing.**

Christians should never revel in violence, but neither should they ignore it. The violence we experience in art might be shocking or even appalling—but perhaps that's not always such a bad thing.

33

# 6

# When Celebrities Preach: A Christian Response

Hollywood celebrities have become the new preachers in American society. It is common for the rich and famous to spend more time on their press tour proclaiming political, religious, and environmental wisdom than they do promoting whatever movie or music album they have recently released. Award shows have become a parade of political lectures rather than a celebration of artistic creation. As increasingly vocal celebrities become the norm, it's important for Christians to understand what this trend means for our society and how we should respond.

## Removing Double Standards

Our first task is to ensure that we don't hold an unfair double standard. Christians frequently lambast Hollywood stars and order them to "just stick to acting" or "just stick to singing." The idea is that famous artists should stay in their lane. But Christians are quick to lavish praise on Christian celebrities who unabashedly proclaim their viewpoints, despite criticizing secular artists for the same behavior.

Christians didn't argue that Tim Tebow should "stick to football" when he appeared in a pro-life Super Bowl ad. When A-list actor Chris Pratt shared about his faith and church on a late-night talk show, Christians applauded him. When Lady Gaga shared her humanistic ideologies on a a similar show, she was crucified.

> If we want a culture that lets Christians use their celebrity influence to share their faith, we must also grant this freedom to those with whom we disagree.

We have a choice. Either free speech and leveraging a celebrity platform is permissible for all or for none. We cannot draw a line and allow only celebrities who support our own beliefs to proclaim their worldview. If we want a culture that lets Christians use their celebrity influence to share their faith, we must also grant this freedom to those with whom we disagree. We might roll our eyes as a 19-year-old pop diva offers her expertise on political policy, human morality, or environmentalism, but she has the right to do so.

## Virtue Signaling and Publicity Stunts

Christians should also be aware that most celebrity preaching has little to do with enacting cultural change. Rarely do celebrities preach an unpopular sermon to an unfavorable congregation. Boldly declaring "love is love" from the stage of the Academy Awards takes as much courage as proclaiming "Jesus loves you" from the pulpit of a First Baptist Church. Most celebrities merely latch onto popular trends and convert them into cultural currency.

In Taylor Swift's VMA acceptance speech for her LGBT anthem "You Need to Calm Down," she declared, "You voting for this video means that you want a world where we're all treated equally under the law regardless of who we love or how we identify!" She might as well have declared, "A vote for me and my art to win awards is a vote for world peace!" The implication seems to be that those who preferred a different artist's video were instead casting their vote for a world of hatred and bigotry ("Good job voting for 'Sucker' by the Jonas Brothers, you despicable racist homophobe!").

A similar example was on display when pop diva Miley Cyrus took a pro-choice stance on Twitter with the provocative slogan, "Don't F— with my Freedom!" The next day, pink sweaters with this "brave" slogan and a gratuitously topless Miley Cyrus went on sale for a tidy sum of $175. The entirety of the money was donated to Planned Parenthood, while Cyrus claimed all the free publicity. As it happens, the political stance conveniently coincided with the marketing push and rollout of her new 3 EP project (with the slogan reappearing in her next radio single). In short, publicly supporting popular ideologies is good for business.

## An Honest Look at Celebrity Power

Much—perhaps *most*—of celebrity preaching is self-serving. At the same time, it's unfair to assume that *all* preaching is merely a marketing tool. Fame does not strip away a celebrity's status as a human being who has genuine hopes, fears, and convictions. Many Christians shake their heads when celebrities speak out about a chosen issue—be it climate change or same-sex marriage—and say, "They're just saying that to be popular." Popularity may indeed be their motivation; but they may also be sincere. Just because celebrities express a belief that we disagree with does not mean they have dubious motives. Thus, as Christians, we should also be aware of celebrities' influence.

Two tendencies become apparent when determining a celebrity's power. The first is that celebrities vastly overestimate the cultural power they wield. The second is that Christians vastly underestimate celebrities' cultural power. Both of these tendencies were on display recently at the Video Music Awards. One of the most buzz-worthy moments of the night was when Taylor Swift looked at her watch and called out the White House to respond to her petition (which she advocated through her award-winning music video). The White House obliged. The next morning, in a brief memo, the White House dismissed the petition, wiping away a year of Swift's political work.

Taylor Swift is arguably the most influential and powerful celebrity in the world right now, but her much-publicized "political awakening" has so far resulted in the political candidate she endorsed losing an election and a petition being dismissed with a shrug. These results should be a reality check for the actual political power celebrities hold.

Taylor Swift's failure to produce actual political change should not, however, trick Christians into assuming that celebrities like her are not producing change. Informed adults are unlikely to reject their established political or religious convictions simply because a young pop star in a flashy outfit tells them to at a gala of the rich and famous. The story changes, however, with the young fan who idolizes a celeb, finds an intimate connection with the artist's music, and is still developing his or her own worldview.

Taylor Swift's song "You Need to Calm Down" failed abysmally at pressuring the government to pass a political bill but was a roaring success at framing the cultural narrative that surrounds that bill. The song draws a clear line between the enlightened (people who agree with Swift) and the ignorant/bigoted (anyone who disagrees with Swift). The consequences of dictating and defining the cultural narrative for a generation of young people will echo for far longer than the passing of a single political bill.

> **The consequences of dictating and defining the cultural narrative for a generation of young people will echo for far longer than the passing of a single political bill.**

the cultural narrative for a generation of young people will echo for far longer than the passing of a single political bill. Many Christians who chuckled at Swift's political failure may have to come to terms with her cultural success when her legion of young fans become the movers and shakers in our society and start proselytizing her gospel that conservative Christians just "need to calm down."

## Final Thoughts

As celebrity preaching becomes more widely accepted (and more commercially profitable), we can expect more and more Hollywood stars to join the chorus. While most of their sermons will never penetrate beyond the Hollywood echo chamber, Christians should be aware of the influence of those that do. Celebrities are producing change. Perhaps not as much change as their egos believe, but change nonetheless. Only time will tell just how deep or wide their influence is, but, regardless, Christians should be ready to meet the secular gospel with the one true Gospel.

# Part Two

# Worldview
# COLLISIONS

# 7

# Is Apologetics a Waste of Time?

"Apologetics is a waste of time."

That was the first comment I received after giving a Sunday School lesson focused on apologetics.

#Awkward.

The sentiment is not uncommon. While apologetics—arguments and justifications in support or defense of the Christian faith—has become more mainstream in recent years, many Christians still have hesitations about it.

"God doesn't need defending," some say. "You can't debate someone into heaven," others argue. Much of this criticism is driven by anti-intellectualism and a conviction that faith concerns the heart, not the mind. I once heard someone say, "We need to *evangelize*, not *apologize*." Put that on a bumper sticker.

Of course, the Church *does* need to evangelize. But, for many people, evangelism has essentially become synonymous with sharing their personal testimony and then asking for a response.

Personal testimonies are one of the most important tools Christians have in sharing the Gospel. But they are not—and *should* not—be the only one. Is apologetics a waste of time? Well, that depends a great deal on what we mean by "apologetics" and how serious we are about reaching a lost world.

## God is More Than Your Story

"Apologetics is a waste of time," my disgruntled listener said. He followed this declaration by stating, "I don't see the point. All we need to do is just tell people what Jesus has done in our life."

To this, I responded, "Stories are powerful. But imagine that I've had a transformative and deeply spiritual experience with hot yoga, which has allowed me to find total peace by putting me in tune with my inner divinity. Isn't it awesome that we've both found spiritual comfort?"

"That's not true comfort."

"Why not? What makes your testimony true but not mine?"

"Because my God is real."

"Says who?"

"Because the Bible was…"

What followed were several classic arguments and justifications for the validity of the biblical God as the one true God. No more than thirty seconds after declaring that apologetics is unnecessary, our conversation hit a wall that apologetics needed to break down.

Apologetics is not just valuable—it's inevitable. Our stories are powerful, and God uses our testimonies to draw unbelievers to Himself. At the same time, if *all* we have is our personal testimony, there is no way to adjudicate between competing stories. Christians are left with the argument, "My God is true because my story is true, and your God is false because *your* story is false—regardless of what you say!"

> **Apologetics is not just valuable—it's inevitable.**

In short, your God is false because your experiences aren't real, and your experiences aren't real because your God is false. Round and round the carousel we go!

## Breaking Down Walls

Apologetics and evangelism are not in conflict. Both—when used properly—work together to point unbelievers toward Christ. Only God can save souls, but, for whatever divine reasons, He chooses to work through humans.

If there is *no* human element involved, then evangelism would be as superfluous as apologetics. Personal evangelism classes at church are a waste of everyone's time if our words and actions are of no consequence. A pastor's words have no power outside of the Holy

Spirit. Nevertheless, pastors should still contemplate scripture, read biblical commentaries, and organize their sermons into a logical and flowing presentation. God's power does not mitigate human responsibility.

Many unbelievers have built emotional or intellectual walls around their heart to resist the Truth. We might have our personal testimony well-rehearsed and ready to go, but our words will fall on deaf ears if those walls stand strong.

> **God's power does not mitigate human responsibility.**

- "It's cool that God has changed your life for the better, but unless you can explain how your *loving* God allows child trafficking to exist, I'm not interested in hearing any more about him."

- "I'm glad your religion makes you happy, but science is clear that life originated from evolution and not creation."

- "Sure, there's some good teaching in the Bible, but wasn't it written years and years after the actual events? Besides, with all the translations and scribal errors, we can't really trust it anyways."

- "What makes *your* Bible true, but not the Quran or Book of Mormon? What gave the medieval church the right to decide when the biblical canon was closed?"

What should Christians do when facing such walls? Turn tail and run? Shrug and declare the challenge too great? Or, like Joshua and the Israelites standing before the fortified city of Jericho, do we bring down the walls? God destroyed the walls that day, but the Israelites marched around the city seven times and blew the trumpets.

> **Unbelievers deserve thoughtful answers to their honest questions about God.**

Unbelievers deserve thoughtful answers to their honest questions about God. Apologetics—by providing these answers—knocks down the intellectual and emotional walls, clearing the way for evangelism to bring the truth of the Gospel straight to their unguarded hearts.

## By All Possible Means

The apostle Paul boldly preached the kingdom of God—but he also stood on the Areopagus and reasoned with the Greek philosophers, using their intellectual arguments, religious beliefs, and cultural artifacts to bridge the chasm of belief between them. He declared, "I have become all things to all people so that *by all possible means* I might save some" (1 Cor. 9:22).

Are we willing to do the same? Our own personal story is comfortable. After all, we're experts on ourselves. How far are we willing to go, however, when unbelievers hunger for assistance outside our comfort zone and area of expertise. Are we willing to study scientific proofs? Dig into philosophical arguments to answer difficult intellectual objections? Examine other religious worldviews to pinpoint their logical and theological inconsistencies?

The Church should be willing to "do its homework" in order to be prepared to "give an answer to everyone who asks you to give the reason for the hope that you have" (1 Peter 3:15). Debate for debate's sake is pointless. Reducing apologetics and Christianity to purely intellectual rhetoric, divorced from the heart and evangelistic foundation, *is* dangerous and wrong.

But we do not have to choose between extremes. Christians do not face an either/or decision between intellectual apologetics and emotional evangelism. We are simply called to spread the Good News to the ends of the earth, and the urgency of this commission should lead us to use any tools at our disposal.

Apologetics is only a waste of time if we believe reaching unbelievers *by all possible means* is a waste of time. For the sake of those still lost in the darkness of their unbelief, I pray that the Church decides otherwise.

# 8

# Darwin Hates Peacocks: How Beauty Shows that God Exists

Charles Darwin's relationship with birds is best classified as "it's complicated." On one hand, Galapagos finches were so pivotal to his theory of evolution that the birds are known as "Darwin's finches." On the other hand, in letter to a colleague, Darwin famously confessed, *"The sight of a feather in a peacock's tail, whenever I gaze at it, makes me sick!"*

There are many "missing links" in the evolutionist's worldview, but arguably none is more conspicuous than the existence of and appreciation for **beauty**. Darwin's famous book, *On the Origin of Species*, ends with the oft-quoted words, *"Endless forms most beautiful and most wonderful have been, and are being, evolved."* This is a fitting end to Darwin's book, as "the beautiful" is also effectively the end of what his theory can explain.

Earlier in the same letter, when Darwin revealed the nauseating effect of peacock tail feathers, he wrote, *"I remember well the time when the thought of the eye made me cold all over, but I have got over this stage of the complaint."* In Darwin's own mind, beauty represented a more formidable and insurmountable problem to his evolutionary theory then even the most difficult biological and scientific hurdles. To understand why, we need a quick crash course on his theory.

Darwinian evolution requires two elements: 1) a struggle for survival (e.g. limited food, etc.) and 2) biological mutations (called adaptions) that provide some individuals an advantage over others. In a simplified sense, a bird might be born with a mutation that gives it a slightly longer beak, allowing it to get the most food. The short-beaked birds, unable to find enough sustenance, will eventually die off. The large-beaked birds then have offspring that share their advantage, and, over a long period of time, the species of bird will all have larger beaks. This phenomenon is called "selective fitness" and is the essence of the mantra "survival of the fittest."

On its own, the theory might appear logical and workable— until *beauty*.

Like Captain Kirk cosplay at a Star Wars convention, beauty is painfully out of place in the theory. Not only does a peacock's brightly colored tail feathers have no survival value, they actually have the opposite effect. The bright feathers are like neon signs declaring to prey, "Here I am! Come eat me!"

The flamboyant Irish poet Oscar Wilde famously wrote, "All Art is quite useless." Part of what makes art *art* is that it requires no functionality. It simply *is*. Beauty serves no purpose beyond being beautiful. We do not stare at a brilliant purple sunset in hopes of learning a practical lesson on how to survive a cruel winter. We do so because the sunset is beautiful and pleasing to watch. No naturalistic worldview has ever been able to adequately explain the "wow" moment that comes from looking at a majestic mountain range or the impulse to pick a pretty flower and smell it.

> The only viable answer to the question of beauty is found not in the natural world but in the heavens.

Evolutionists have gone to great lengths to force beauty to fit into Darwinism, incessantly hammering a square peg into a circular hole. Darwin's own solution to the problem was so far outside the framework of his evolutionary theory (and so baseless) that even the majority of his own followers lambasted him. Some even called him a traitor to his own theory! Thus, in a humorous turn of events, Darwin was deemed not to be Darwinian enough to be a Darwinist! Even today, evolutionists are still desperately trying to solve this old riddle of beauty, oblivious to the fact that their efforts are in vain. The only viable answer to the question of beauty is found not in the natural world but in the heavens.

The Bible reveals, "The heavens declare the glory of God; the skies proclaim the work of his hands" (Psalm 19:1). God did not create a purely functional universe. He also made it beautiful. He did not merely create an environment suited and balanced for survival. He also filled it with enchanting colors and sublime landscapes. Beauty did not evolve; it was given as an amazing gift. Even 150 years after Darwin has passed on, the sight of a peacock's tail feathers is still enough to make his followers sick.

# 9

# "I Just Can't Believe in a God Who Would…"

Last year, a survey by Pew Research Center revealed that 44% of Americans don't believe in God as described by the Christian Bible.[6]

That number is sobering.

Skeptics reject the existence of God for countless reasons, some based on intellect, others on emotion, and most on a messy mixture of both. One of the most popular reasons people give for their disbelief is, "I just can't believe in a God who would…" They complete the statement in any number of ways:

"…send people to hell."

"…condemn homosexuality."

"...let evil things happen to children."

"...let my aunt die from cancer."

"...allow that hurricane to hit Florida."

You've probably heard variations of this reasoning. Perhaps you've made similar statements yourself. But beneath the surface, this logic is anything but logical.

Skeptics often accuse Christians of being wishful thinkers who cling to faith in God as an emotional crutch. (Karl Marx said, "Religion is the opium of the people.") God, they say, is whoever Christians need Him to be. But an authentic biblical faith demands the opposite view. When Moses stood before the burning bush, he was terrified, confused, and cynical about God's instructions. Far from adapting to Moses' concerns, God declared, "I AM WHO I AM" (Exodus 3:14). Love Him or hate Him, agree or disagree, God proclaims that *I am* who *I've been* and who *I always will be.*

On the other hand, skeptics who assert, "I just can't believe in a God who would..." take the opposite view. They begin with their own emotional wishes, standards, and desires and refuse to accept anything that falls short of their criteria. In other words, Christians adapt themselves to God, while skeptics adapt God to themselves.

Today's culture gives lip service to a postmodernist worldview (ex. "Truth is subjective. What's true for me is true for me, and what's true for you is true for you."), but this nonsensical philosophy crumbles the moment the worldview requires action. To say, "There is no absolute truth" is, of course, a statement of absolute truth—akin to Obi-Wan Kenobi telling his fallen pupil, "Only a Sith speaks in absolutes," which is itself an absolute statement.

As the father of two young boys, I have often thought, "I can't believe a father would physically harm his children." Tragically, I understand that abusive fathers do exist, and they exist whether I understand them or not. I can abhor them, refuse to associate with them, and protest them, but I cannot simply "wish" them away (regardless of how badly I wish I could).

This is a fact: either God exists or He doesn't. Our feelings about His moral character or actions can't change this reality.

When people say, "I just can't believe in a God who would…" they mean, "I hate any God who would let my mother die in a car accident," or "Any God who sends good people to hell is a monster and not worthy of my worship." They don't mean they *can't* believe but that they *won't* believe. Not that they *don't* believe but that they *don't want to* believe. In this way, atheist philosopher Thomas Nagel should be commended for his transparency when he wrote, "It isn't just that I don't believe in God and, naturally, hope that I'm right in my belief. It's that I hope there is no God! I don't want there to be a God; I don't want the universe to be like that."[7]

> **Fortunately, God's existence doesn't depend on our limited human thinking and ever-changing opinions. Indeed, His unchanging nature is part of what makes Him God.**

Next time you hear someone say, "I just can't believe in a God who would…" pause, look beneath the surface, and be sensitive to the real truth behind the statement. Many people today hate God. But it's difficult to hate something that doesn't exist. Fortunately, God's existence doesn't depend on our limited human thinking and ever-changing opinions. Indeed, His unchanging nature is part of what makes Him God.

# 10

# Why Christians Are Debating People into Hell

We live in an argumentative culture. And social media platforms like Facebook and Twitter have—for better or worse—made it easier than ever to find a dance partner. Christians have been equally as caught up in the argumentative aura.

Christian apologetics—the discipline of defending and providing proofs for the faith—has exploded in popularity in recent years. Movies like *God's Not Dead* and countless "apologetic handbooks" have helped thrust the discipline, once reserved for the ivory tower philosophers, into the mainstream.

Much good has come from this shift. One of the foremost reasons young adults abandon their faith after high school is that they were repeatedly told *what* to believe but never helped to understand *why* to believe it.

Unfortunately, however, with the good comes a danger for abuse. Despite being well-intentioned, I worry that we've lost our way.

In the Church's zeal to equip Christians with a quiver full of apologetic arguments and proofs, we have neglected to teach them how to wield the bow or why we shoot at all. We've provided the content but have not established the necessary foundation—the right character, heart, and purpose of apologetic discourse.

> " One of the foremost reasons young adults abandon their faith after high school is that they were repeatedly told what to believe but never helped to understand why to believe it. "

## Mischaracterizing People

Many contemporary apologetic approaches operate on the assumption that people are primarily rational beings. Thus, if a skeptic remains skeptical, the obvious solution is to provide more and more rational evidence until the person crosses the threshold into faith.

But people are *not* primarily rational beings. In an age where biological sex is rejected in favor of subjective feeling and "sexual identity," it's valid to wonder if we're even rational beings at all. The truth is that we are not rational but *emotional* beings.

We use our rationality to prop up the convictions of our heart, not the other way around. Reason may be the roadway, but emotion is the gateway—and it tends to allow entry only to that which is already abundantly present on the other side of the door.

There are plenty of very convincing intellectual arguments for the existence of God, but not all intellectuals are convinced.

There are many scientific proofs for God, but not all scientists acknowledge them.

The Christian apologist's task, therefore, is not just to fill up minds with more knowledge but to soften hardened hearts that suffocate and blind skeptics to the knowledge and evidence already present all around them. When apologetics becomes an intellectual game, divorced from its emotional and evangelistic foundation, the venture is doomed before it has even begun.

## A Distorted Purpose

The disproportionate emphasis on intellectualism and rationality presents an all-too-alluring slippery slope into abuse. Many Christians today take an almost vindictive delight in "owning" or "demolishing" the opposition and their pitiful worldviews. Apologetics becomes a game of intellectual chess, and Christians are determined to claim the victory at all costs.

But the purpose of apologetics should never be to make a skeptic look foolish or to tear an unbeliever down. The proper purpose is to help guide unbelievers to the doorstep of belief, to inch them ever closer toward the freedom that comes from Christ alone.

Too often as Christians we rush off to celebrate our "victory" in the intellectual debate, all the while leaving our "devastated" or "owned" opponents lost further down the chasm of atheism than they were before. That result is an abject failure, regardless of what the debate scorecard says. Indeed, when the apostle Paul debated and reasoned with the Jewish leaders or the Gentile philosophers, he had just one driving purpose, and it certainly wasn't to "destroy" or "own" his opponents.

There should be mourning, not cheering, when a skeptic continues along the path to hell. The Facebook arguments we won or "Twitter owns" will surely be far from our mind when we one day reach heaven, but the sinners we loved and guided to the foot of the cross will stand alongside us and join their voice to ours in praising God.

Why, then, have so many Christians so wholly embraced the argumentative attitude that defines our culture? I believe that somewhere along the way we've lost our faith in the power of love and grace. We've grown tired of turning the other cheek, and we're ready to start hitting back. We're fed up with being called unintellectual and ignorant, so—like Katniss at the end of *The Hunger Games*—we're out for blood and yearn to watch others suffer the same indignity we have endured.

> **The unbelieving world does not bat an eye at "clever Christians," but it stands back in astonishment when the Church demonstrates the reckless and inexplicable love of Christ.**

## For The Love of Christ Compels Us

In the midst of this tempest of self-serving desires, however, we cannot lose sight of the fact that the power to transform our lost and broken world is not the intellectual genius of Christians, but the everlasting love of Christ. The unbelieving world does not bat an eye at "clever Christians," but it stands back in astonishment when the Church demonstrates the reckless and inexplicable love of Christ.

Christians should use any and every tool at our disposal, including intellectual arguments and rational proofs. I've seen many Christians' faith strengthened and many unbelievers' skepticism wane as a result of this apologetic approach. I'm not suggesting that we don't need apologetics, merely that we require love and grace far more. There is a proper time and place for both. But if we must choose only one—or if the former ever begins to infringe on the latter—the Christian must always choose the path of love. After all, love and patience will always be a more compelling and powerful case for Christ than fast-talking arguments and clever intellectual rhetoric.

> **Love and patience will always be a more compelling and powerful case for Christ than fast-talking arguments and clever intellectual rhetoric.**

# Part Three

# CHURCH
# COLLISIONS

# 11

# Why Creative Young Adults Are Abandoning the Church (and What We Can Do About It)

Consider two realities:

A) Millennials and Gen Z are routinely defined as more creative minded and arts oriented than previous generations.

B) Millennials and Gen Z are abandoning the Church at higher rates than ever before.

Now ask yourself this question: is there any connection between these two realities? According to several recent studies and books (including *You Lost Me* by David Kinnaman and *Meet Generation Z* by James Emery White), the answer is *yes*. Young adults are abandoning the Church at alarming rates, and the creative minded—the *creatives*—make up a substantial portion of this exile.

# Why Are They Leaving?

There is not a single reason why so many creative young adults are leaving the Church in the same way there is no solitary reason why Americans love to watch football. To speak about a certain "generation" is always to speak about a mass of individuals, each with unique and personal stories. But from working with young people—particularly with creatives— and by studying many of the current resources available, I've notice three general trends.

## 1. **They are Bored**

Contrary to popular assumptions, the majority of young adults who leave the Church are not necessarily doctrinally opposed to Christianity or angry at the Church. Statistically, most do so simply because they are *bored* (31% of churched 18-29-year-olds describe the Church as "boring"). Creatives are naturally among the dissatisfied, as church services are generally conducted with a left-brain mentality that appeals to rationality and knowledge rather than emotion or imagination.

## 2. **They Feel Restricted**

More than 13% of 18-29-year-olds express that the Church does not provide opportunities for creative people. This statistic represents *all* types of young adults—jocks, scientists, mathematicians, etc. When limited to the young adults most affected by the issue—the creatives themselves—that number skyrockets. In fact, after surveying thousands of young adults, David Kinnaman—president of the Barna Group— concluded that there is a widespread consensus among young adults that the Church is a "creativity killer." When the arts—or at least music—*are* present in church worship, they are often seen as lacking innovation (we sing the same song for 10 years) and listless. While the budding young creatives are often willing to volunteer, rarely—if ever—do they find their participation artistically challenging or fulfilling.

### 3. **They Feel Out of Place**

Creatives are naturally disposed to wander. Art has always invited the exploration of new ideas and questioning of the status quo. Artists regularly live on the front lines of their culture, which means they are often among the first casualties. Yet, many churched creatives feel isolated. As many as 1 in 4 young adults bemoan that the Church is overly negative or unaccepting of the importance of the creative arts and, by

> " **Christians cannot allow the secular world to act as better stewards of our young adults' God-given gifts than the Church is.**

extension, of them. In other words, creative young Christians are among the most likely candidates to be seduced by the world and also among the least discipled by or plugged into the Church.

## What Can the Church Do About It?

### 1. **Stimulate Them**

The Church needs to do a better job of engaging its creatives in ways that stimulate them on an emotional, imaginative, and artistic level. Creativity is a core aspect of the emerging generation's identity. It is not just something they *do*; it is something they *are*. This creative compulsion craves an avenue of expression and engagement. If the Church cannot provide this avenue—worse yet, if the Church represses or prohibits it—creatives will inevitably search elsewhere. Christians cannot allow the secular world to act as better stewards of our young adults' God-given gifts than the Church is.

## 2. **Disciple Them**

The Church should disciple creatives *as creatives*, helping them grow both in their faith and in their craft. Many creative young people drift away from the Church because they want to use their talents to make a positive difference in the world, and the Church doesn't always foster that desire. We need to instill in them an understanding that their gifts are valuable beyond their weekly participation on a praise band. The Church needs to raise up its creatives as vital contributors and disciples, missionaries commissioned and sent out into a crucial, predominantly secular area of culture. Too often, however, we are merely content to let them volunteer once a week to strum simple guitar chords for a few worship songs. If we want to keep creatives in the Church, we must challenge them with a bigger vision, disciple them until they have the faith and character to handle that challenge, then provide the support they need to pursue it wholeheartedly.

## 3. **Love Them**

Let's be honest. Creatives are a strange breed. They can be quirky and difficult to understand. But the Church cannot afford to give up on them. J. R. R. Tolkien famously wrote, "Not all who wander are lost." Creatives might

> **It is much harder to walk away from a loving family.**

confuse us or act in ways that seems strange, but they are family, and the family bond transcends personality types or dispositions. Seek out the creatives in your church. Find ways to love them and support their creative calling. It is easy to walk away from a church. It is much harder to walk away from a loving family.

## Final Thoughts

The Church should not become an art gallery; the sermon should not be delivered as a hip-hop dance, and the meditative invitational song does not require a blazing Zeppelin-esque guitar solo. But the Church *must* be a place where young artists, hip-hop dancers, and electric guitar players are active and contributing members of the family. God created the human brain with a right and left hemisphere, and the body cannot function as fully intended without both present and operating. So too with the Church body. To be a fully functioning church, we need our young creatives, and the first step to achieving this objective is to do whatever it takes to keep them from leaving.

# 12

# Finding Faith in a Perfect King, Not His Imperfect Champions

*"It is better to take refuge in the Lord than to trust in humans. It is better to take refuge in the Lord than to trust in princes."* — Psalm 118:8-9

We live in the age of superheroes. The Hollywood box office reflects the world's enduring captivation with extraordinary individuals. Five of the six highest-grossing films in 2018 were superhero movies. The unprecedented dominance of the genre reveals something important about human nature. We desire champions—mighty men and women who embody our ideal virtues and fight the battles we are unable or unwilling to fight ourselves. We glorify superheroes on the silver screen, because deep down we yearn for superheroes in the real world.

> **We glorify superheroes on the silver screen, because deep down we yearn for superheroes in the real world.**

Christians are not immune to this desire. Almost every month, a new story makes the rounds on social media: "This celebrity is a Christian!" or "This accomplished athlete thanks God for his success!" The zeal to herald famous individuals as Christian champions is, in part, a desperate yearning for affirmation. "Look at this cool rock star! And this famous actor! And this superstar athlete! They're all cool. They're all popular. They're all famous. And they're all on *our* team!"

There is nothing innately wrong with this enthusiasm. We should celebrate whenever anyone places his or her faith in Jesus. Christians should diligently pray for and support individuals who courageously leverage their God-given platform to glorify Christ. At the same time, there is a danger in placing our faith in Christian champions, regardless of how valiant they appear. That Christians often celebrate all the more when the champion is famous and renowned suggests that we are perhaps not that different from the Israelites who declared, "Appoint a king to lead us, such as all the other nations have" (1 Sam. 8:5).

The Israelites had access to an all-powerful God, but they wanted a human champion to "go out before us and fight our battles" (1 Sam. 8:20). As God said to Samuel, "They have rejected me as their king" (1 Sam. 8:7). The Israelites chose Saul for the role because he had the appearance of a king and warrior; he was "as handsome a young man as could be found anywhere in Israel, and he was a head taller than anyone else" (1 Sam. 9:2). Yet, when the ferocious Philistine champion Goliath towered before the Israelite army and mocked their God, Saul was not the best-equipped person to challenge the giant. A young, unknown shepherd boy was.

In the same way, Christians often use irrelevant criteria when electing champions. Athletic talent, a beautiful singing voice, or a successful acting career do not, in their own right, indicate that a person is qualified to be a spokesperson for the faith.

In 2019, breakout Christian singer/songwriter Lauren Daigle sparked controversy when, during a radio interview, she gave wishy-washy answers to questions about the biblical view of homosexuality. Many Christians voiced their disappointment and betrayal. But the emotionally charged fallout was the result of more than her flimsy answers. The real issue was that Daigle had been designated (not of her own doing) as a Christian champion, and, in the eyes of many, she had failed to live up to that responsibility. Christians chose the 27-year-old singer as their champion due to her musical talent and newfound celebrity status and were subsequently shocked to discover that she was not a polished theologian or articulate spokesperson for biblical morality. Like the Israelites, we put our faith in a human rather than God and were inevitably disappointed when she fell short.

Similarly, a well-known actress recently made a passing reference to "faith" during a talk show interview. The next morning, social media buzzed with posts bearing headlines like these: "____ takes a stand for God in Hollywood!" and "The unwavering faith of ____!" Two days later, that same actress went viral in a video filled with profanity and crude humor. The earlier posts unceremoniously stopped making the rounds. I am not making a judgement on this actress or Daigle, both of whom may well have an intimate relationship with Christ. These examples, along with many others, simply demonstrate how quick Christians are to appoint new champions.

Christians should celebrate whenever someone takes a stand for Christ. But, above all, they should remember not to place their faith in human champions but at the feet of the Divine King. The Christian faith requires no celebrity endorsement; it does not depend on popularity or trends. God reigns on His heavenly throne when His subjects are faithful and when they are faithless.

> " The Christian faith requires no celebrity endorsement; it does not depend on popularity or trends. God reigns on His heavenly throne when His subjects are faithful and when they are faithless. "

The world does not need to see that famous people can be Christians. They need to see Christ. From the beginning of human history until now, God has delighted in using the most unexpected and unspectacular people to represent Him to the world—fishermen, tax collectors, slaves, teenagers, carpenters, shepherd boys, prostitutes, cowards, and stuttering speakers. When we become focused only on the representatives, it is time to lift our eyes to the mighty king they represent. He is God, and He alone does not—and *will* not—disappoint.

# 13

## The Reason Why Christians Are So Messed Up and Hypocritical

#ChristianPrivilege

The recently trending hashtag is another sign of a widespread cultural dissatisfaction with Christianity and the Church. Christianity gets a bad rap in today's society, much of it justified. Actress and comedian Sarah Silverman added more kindling to the fire by sharing a shocking sermon snippet on Twitter that depicts a preacher brashly declaring from the pulpit that he hopes, "God breaks her teeth out and she dies." Whenever the word "Christian" appears across social media platforms, it is increasingly followed by other pointed words: hateful, intolerant, bigoted, fake, greedy, corrupt, childish, and so on.

Of all the contemptuous words, perhaps the one that has historically been most zealously lobbed against Christians is *hypocrites*. "Christians claim to be holier, more moral, and more loving," they say, "but in reality, they're no better than the rest of us." This complaint is the baseline of the #ChristianPrivilege hashtag. If Christians are no different than anyone else, why should they get any special privileges? The world looks at the Church and draws this scathing conclusion: Christians are really messed up.

And do you know what? They're absolutely right. Christians *are* really messed up.

In fact, that's the point.

There is an odd notion today that the truth or falsehood of a god hinges on the actions and character of his followers. "How can there be a god," asks the skeptic, "when all his professed followers are so totally messed up?" But this approach is akin to looking through the wrong end of the telescope.

> **What sets Christians apart from the rest of the world is not the absence of illness but the acceptance of a remedy. *The* remedy.**

To assume that the existence of hypocritical, mean-spirited Christians somehow invalidates the Christian faith is to miss the point of Christianity completely. If Christians were not so thoroughly messed up, the Christian religion would not need the Cross and crucifixion. The Christian faith is built on the foundational belief that every person on Earth is so utterly messed up that a holy and perfect God had to send His own beloved Son down from heaven to take on our sin and die in our place.

What sets Christians apart from the rest of the world is not the absence of illness but the acceptance of a remedy. *The* remedy. Christians attend church not to present themselves as perfect, but to declare that they are far from perfect and in desperate need of God's grace and help. This wonderful and beautiful acknowledgment is what allows Christians to sing, "Amazing Grace, how sweet the sound, that saved *a wretch* like me!"

We do not judge a god by the testimony of his followers; we measure his followers by the testimony of their god. If Christians act spiteful, self-centered, or unloving—as many unfortunately do—we must look first at what God commands in the Bible and then measure the actions of his followers against that standard.

I am not implying that the Church should make light of or be apathetic toward these abuses, but that these shortcomings reflect the sinful nature of man, not the holy character of God. Christians should be leading the cultural charge to stamp out injustice and call out the sinful distortion within our midst, but we should also recognize that human sin—no matter how abhorrent and tragic—will never infringe on the perfect, holy nature of God.

The unbelieving world is absolutely correct. Christians are not perfect —and that is okay. Our imperfection is a prerequisite for God to demonstrate His amazing and boundless grace. The powerful testimony of the Church is not that perfect Christians love God, but that a perfect God loves messed up Christians. The difference between these

> " **Christianity has *nothing* to do with perfect Christians and *everything* to do with a perfect Christ.** "

two perspectives makes all the difference in the world. In short, Christianity has *nothing* to do with perfect Christians and *everything* to do with a perfect Christ.

# 14

# Unashamed of the Church

Is it easier today to be unashamed of Jesus or His church?

Pop star Lady Gaga made headlines (you don't say!) for her scathing remarks about Vice-President Mike Pence: "You are the worst representation of what it means to be a Christian." Gaga's concern was not that Pence poorly represented traditional Christian beliefs but that he represented the wrong version of Christianity.

The next day CNN ran the headline, "Christianity's future looks more like Lady Gaga than Mike Pence." The article pitted progressive Christianity against fundamentalist Christianity. New school against old school. Tradition against progression. The dividing line between these opposing "versions" of Christianity was not Jesus but the Church.

Jesus is not a hard man to love (obedience to all He taught is, of course, another matter entirely). He preached love as the greatest commandment, showed compassion to social outcasts, and demanded care for widows and orphans. Even in a modern culture that largely rejects His claims of divinity, Jesus (as a man) remains an ideal and symbol to strive toward. In short, people are mostly okay with Jesus— just so long as He doesn't come bundled with the baggage of His church.

This mindset is not reserved only for Hollywood celebrities or atheists. Several years ago, a spoken word poem, "Why I Hate Religion, But Love Jesus," went viral on YouTube and now has more than 34 million views. More recently, the hashtag #ImAChristianBut was trending on Twitter, completed in various ways:

...I'm not homophobic.

...I'm not intolerant.

...I'm not close minded.

...I'm accepting of other people's religions.

Last year, a Barna survey found that roughly 10% of Americans fall into the category, "Love Jesus but not the Church."[8] I witnessed this phenomenon first hand when I asked a classroom of nearly 40 students, ranging from grades 9-12, if they believed that the Church was an important part of the Christian faith. Only three raised their hands.

Ironically, even churches themselves occasionally criticize and downplay the Church's relevancy. I've visited several church plants that leveraged this general dissatisfaction and distaste for the Church (capital C) as their primary marketing tool for their own church (small c): "Many of you have been disenchanted and let down by the Church," the pastor would say. "But we are not like *those* churches." The message, intentional or not, seems to be that the traditional Church is broken beyond repair, and it is long past time for something new.

A popular Christian catchphrase is, "It's not a religion; it's a relationship." This theology is sound, but this creed has unintentionally offered a backdoor for embarrassed Christians to escape. If all we need is Jesus, why bother with the headache, scorn, and negative stigma of the Church?

In his second letter to Timothy, the apostle Paul makes an interesting plea: "Do not be ashamed for the testimony about our Lord or of me his prisoner. Rather, join with me in suffering for the gospel, by the power of God" (1:8). Paul is not telling Timothy to be unashamed of the Gospel (he says that elsewhere), but to be unashamed of *the testimony about* Christ. Paul, writing from a jail cell in Rome, was troubled that so many Christians were abandoning the early church teaching and leaders. Within the first few years of the Church, many believers were ready to give up on it and embrace other more culturally acceptable religious teachings.

> **To love Christ is to love the Church.**

Paul understood that to be unashamed of Jesus is also to be unashamed of His church. When trying to find the strongest manifestation of love, Paul wrote, "Love . . . just as Christ loved the church and gave himself up for her"

(Ephesians 5:25). To "love Jesus but not the Church" may be an option in a survey poll, but it is not an option Jesus has offered. When the apostle Peter declared his love for Jesus three times, Jesus responded, "Feed my lambs." "Take care of my sheep." "Feed my sheep." To love Jesus was to love His people. To love Christ is to love the Church.

Churches are not infallible. When the Church stumbles and strays from its calling, Christians must be ready to correct and repair. This restoration cannot happen from the outside. Christians must be in the Church. They must love the Church as Jesus did. The Church has always been Jesus' plan. To reject the Church as a failure says as much about what we think of Jesus as it does our opinion of the Church. God did not make a mistake in establishing the Church. It is and will always be imperfect because it is filled with imperfect Christians. Yet, it is against the dark backdrop of our imperfections that the light of a perfect God shines all the brighter.

> **The Church has always been Jesus' plan. To reject the Church as a failure says as much about what we think of Jesus as it does our opinion of the Church.**

# 15

# A Challenge to The Complaining Christian

I had a dog named Chevy as a child. He was a spunky little guy whose favorite activity was to sit halfway up the staircase, positioned with a view out the front door window, and bark at anything that moved. No one ever reciprocated his impassioned calls. In fact, few likely even heard his high-pitched yaps. This lack of recognition did not stop him from barking and barking and barking. He'd bark until his voice grew hoarse and then bark some more.

Chevy is an apt metaphor for contemporary culture. Indeed, Chevy's scruffy face would arguably make a better Twitter icon than the little blue bird. We live in a culture in which many people talk, but few people pay attention. Many people bark until their throats grow raspy, but few get up off the stairs to do anything about it. In short, we live in a complaining culture. This negativity is evident in the unbelieving world and, sadly, the Church as well.

# Why Do We Complain?

If complaints fixed problems, America would be a utopia. So why do we keep complaining? For at least three reasons:

1. ***Because We Are Self-Centered Humans***. We started complaining in the Garden of Eden and haven't stopped since.

2. ***Because We Can***. Social media allows us to join a hashtag movement and repost an inflammatory click-bait headline (for an article we likely didn't read), all from the comfort of our couch while eating popcorn and watching the big game.

3. ***Because We Feel Helpless***. The world is messed up. Crazy ideologies that would have drawn unreserved laughter a few years ago are now policed by the zealots of the cancel culture machine. We want to make a change, but we feel powerless—so we complain. To anyone who will listen (and to those who won't). We complain to family and friends, and we complain to random strangers in the comments section.

## Going Beyond Complaints

As Facebook and Twitter demonstrate, the epidemic of contagious complaining is not unique to Christians. It is a cultural plague. But as the Church, secular culture is not our standard—Christ is.

> **Our constant complaints reveal more about our view of God than they do about the state of today's culture.**

As the wider culture jumps aboard the boycott bandwagon,

the Church must demonstrate— through our actions and not just our voices—that constant complaining is not the only option. It is far easier to boycott something than it is to offer a better solution. It takes less energy to attack an existing idea than it does to present an attractive alternative. The Facebook memes that flood our timelines will not make a lasting difference in the world, but a love-fueled proclamation and demonstration of the Gospel in our lives will.

## Offering A Better Alternative

As Christians, the temptation to complain is real, but the justification to do so is not. Christians are not *just* selfish humans; we are also new creations. Christians have access to all the same technological avenues to voice our complaints as the world does, but we are not called to live as the world lives. Most importantly, Christians may feel helpless, but we are *not* helpless. The same sovereign God who has reigned upon His heavenly throne throughout eternity is not suddenly stumped or tongue-tied by the divisiveness of 2019 America. Our constant complaints reveal more about our view of God than they do about the state of today's culture.

Too often as Christians we give lip-service that God is in control but act as though the eternal king's throne resides in the White House rather than the heavens. We declare that God is all-powerful but spend more time participating in the latest hashtag movement than praying for God's power to be poured out. We sing that the victory

> **Our complaints suggest a lack of faith that God is in control and an impatience with His perfect timing.**

is already won but act as though the devil is gaining ground. Our complaints suggest a lack of faith that God is in control and an impatience with His perfect timing.

> **The world should know us not only by what outrages us but by what fills us with inexplicable joy in the face of an outrageous culture.**

To be clear, I'm not implying that the Church should remain silent. For, even though extremists have sent the social justice movement off the tracks, social concerns and injustice are fundamentally Christian concerns. Christians *should* be upset by much of what they see happening in culture. In fact, perhaps we should be *more* upset—enough to spur us to stop barking, get off the stairs, and join God's activity and work to redeem our messed-up world.

Christians should be *for* God more than just *against* culture. The world should know us not only by what outrages us but by what fills us with inexplicable joy in the face of an outrageous culture. In short, we owe the world far more than our complaints. Thankfully, as Christians, we have something far more valuable to offer instead.

Part Four

# Reviews

# 16

## Joker (Movie Review)

*A Complicated but Ultimately Empty Film.*

### About the Film

Talking about this movie is like jogging a brisk 5K race through a minefield. *Joker* is perhaps the most talked about and buzz-worthy movie of the year—and not always for positive reasons. On one hand, some critics and viewers have dubbed the movie a masterpiece. On the other hand, some viewers and media outlets have hysterically condemned it as a "danger to society." But in the end, *Joker* turns out to be neither.

This film is as much a mixed bag as any movie I've reviewed this year. The doomsday-level panic this film has raised is grossly misplaced; but, it is certainly not a masterpiece or monumental film either. *Joker* exists—much like its titular character—in a messy and largely unsatisfactory no-man's land between these two extremes.

From a technical and cinematic standpoint, *Joker* is an expertly crafted film. The cinematography is inventive and consistently interesting, the music is phenomenal, and Joaquin Phoenix is mesmerizing in the title role. He absolutely deserves to be enshrined alongside the late Heath Ledger in the "Joker Hall of Fame." But the main problem with the film is that, beneath these outwardly captivating elements, it feels utterly empty.

*Joker* frequently charges into serious thematic material but seldom has much of interest or worth to say. Like many "gritty" R-Rated films, it too often mistakes "dark" and "disturbing" for mature or insightful. The film echoes Wyldstyle, in *The Lego Movie*, who declares, "Batman's a true artist. Dark. Brooding…" Of course, there is nothing necessarily wrong with telling a dark or disturbing story. But *Joker* uses many of these moments in the way a horror flick uses cheap "jump-scares." It goes out of its way at disturbing viewers with the slow-building horror on screen, but it overreaches and, in doing so, divorces itself from the human element that this film deeply needed. It may not be the "dangerous" movie many have declared it to be, but I don't think it's a film that society needs right now. In the end, *Joker*—and the conversations surrounding it—is much ado about nothing.

## For Consideration

**On the Surface—(Profanity, Sexual Content, Violence, etc.).**
*Profanity:* Frequent F-words and other profanities.

*Sexuality:* A few minor suggestive moments, but nothing gratuitous.

*Violence:* Several graphic moments of bloody violence and death. The violence is treated with justified weight and seriousness, but this is certainly not your typical and sanitized "superhero violence."

## Beneath the Surface— (Themes, Philosophical Messages, Worldview, etc.)

### 1. Mental Health

The film shines a light on the issue of mental health and exposes the dangerous and harmful mistreatment and fear society frequently has toward the mentally ill. While I commend the film for delving into this important issue, I'm not sure it's doing so is beneficial. In the film, Arthur Fleck (the eventual "Joker") is a severely mentally ill individual. The illness he suffers from is never identified, but it encompasses a growing number of conditions. Fleck lacks empathy, is obsessive, delusional, angry, depressed, and even suffers from uncontrollable laughter (although this last condition is somewhat vague). In a sense, Fleck has the burden of embodying all mental illness in an almost metaphorical way. As a result, *Joker* doesn't really offer meaningful insight into any of them.

*Joker* does not have a clearly defined or articulated "message" or "moral." But a main point of emphasis is seemingly to expose the mistreatment of the mentally ill and, as a result, to inspire viewers to be more empathetic and compassionate toward them. Yet, *Joker* largely undercuts itself. If anything, *Joker* reaffirms the very myth it wants to dispel. Arthur Fleck is not a sympathetic character. Nor is he even a realistic portrayal of mental illness. Rather, Fleck is an exaggerated case of psychopathic behavior. Throughout the film, Fleck is a ticking time bomb. While increased compassion from the Gotham citizens may have delayed his eventual "snap," his turn to "the Joker" feels inevitable. Gotham does not "break" Fleck as much as it "exposes" him. If Joker represents the mentally ill, then society *should* be fearful and unnerved. "Be nice to the mentally ill so that they don't become psychopaths and kill you" is not an inspiring or helpful message.

A moment in my theater effectively captured my sentiments. In the scene, a fearful dwarf is attempting to leave a room after an instance of shocking violence. But the door is deadbolted, and, due to his short stature, he is unable to reach the lock and escape. Despite the weightiness of the scene, many people in my theater were laughing. I can't speak on behalf of those struggling with mental illness, but at least for me, I don't think the film handled its theme in a respectful way. Instead, it seems to use mental health as a plot device to prop up its fictional story rather than using its story to speak about mental health.

## Final Verdict

The Joker is a confusing character, and *Joker* is a confusing film. No, this film—despite the hysteria—is not going to compel audiences to go buy clown masks and rebel against society. If we fearfully and rashly believe that a two-hour movie is enough to transform audiences into dangerous psychopathic monsters, the problem is with us and not the film. At the same time, I don't think *Joker* is nearly as profound or stimulating as it thinks it is. Joaquin Phoenix's performance is arguably worth the price of admission, but I'm not sure there's much value or depth to the film beyond that. Its greatest success may have been to start a cultural conversation about mental health and the power of film to influence culture. Unfortunately, much like the film itself, I worry that these conversations will be more destructive than constructive. Like the guilty thrill of watching a car accident from the side of the road, *Joker* is captivating to watch but offers little in return.

While I know there will be many people out there who *love* this film, I can't recommend it. My best advice is that if you're at all on the fence and concerned about what you've seen and heard about it, skip it. This is not the type of movie that will surprise or convince a viewer who does not already enjoy dark, gritty films. But if you have enjoyed similar movies, you will likely enjoy it more than I did.

# 17

# Taylor Swift—"Lover" (Music Review)

Taylor Swift's highly acclaimed new album *Lover* is one of the most worshipful and religious offerings I've heard in years. It's also one of the most depressing and hopeless. *Lover* is a zealous and unabashed worship album to her god—love.

## The Artist

Taylor Swift has never been a deep songwriter. She rocketed into the superstar stratosphere on the back of her whimsical (and occasionally vindictive) tunes about romance and heartbreak. In the beginning, there was an undeniably endearing quality to these tracks (if you pretend that you didn't give her 2008 album *Fearless* repeated plays back in the day, you're a liar). While she has radically altered her musical style in recent albums, *Lover* proves that her lyrical themes and inspiration have evaded similar progression. Only a handful of tracks on *Lover* venture out from the safe haven of love and romance in a half-hearted attempt to explore new topics and themes (and without much success). But what was endearing as a naïve 17-year-old loses much of its glimmer when performed by a 29-year-old. This immaturity sets the stage for a largely harrowing and empty album that not even catchy, bubblegum-pop melodies can rescue.

## The Album

*Lover* kicks off with the catchy, upbeat anthem, "I Forgot That You Existed." It's a little hard to get past the irony that the countless hours Swift spent writing and recording a song that she will sing on tour for years to come indicates that her memory is perhaps not as poor as she lets on (but I digress). More importantly, the song establishes the tone for the rest of the album, in which Swift looks back on failed love, celebrates current love, and dreams of future love. Similar romance-themed songs follow with "Lover," "The Archer," "I Think He Knows," and "Paper Rings." By the time the album reaches track nine, "Cornelia Street," Swift's obsession with love starts to become concerning and depressing.

"Cornelia Street"—the best musical track on the album—is the first song in which Swift's religious affiliation is explicit. After reminiscing about a long-gone romance, she sings "That became my religion, listen." *Love* is Swift's religion, and she remains devout despite experiencing continual dissatisfaction. The next song, "Death by a Thousand Cuts," includes lyrics about getting drunk but still being unable to overcome the pain of broken relationships. By the time the album reaches track 13, even Swift acknowledges that her religion is a fantasy. The chorus of the song fittingly titled "False God" (which is perhaps the weakest on the entire album) goes like this:

"But we might just get away with it
Religion's in your lips
Even if it's a false god
We'd still worship
We might just get away with it
The altar is my hips
Even if it's a false god
We'd still worship this love."

A later song "Afterglow" sees Swift lamenting and taking blame for yet another broken relationship. The penultimate song, "It's Nice to Have a Friend," is reminiscent of her hit song "Love Story" (although not nearly as catchy) in that it weaves a narrative of a storybook romance. This idealistic romance is assumedly the one Swift herself continues to yearn for.

The album ends with the song "Daylight." It expresses a desperate hope that Swift has finally found solace and peace in her chosen religion. The lyrics begin with the refrain, **"My love was as cruel as the cities I've lived in."** In contrast, the chorus rings out:

**"I don't wanna look at anything else now that I saw you.
I don't wanna think of anything else now that I thought of you.
I've been sleeping so long in a 20-year dark night.
And now I see daylight, I only see daylight."**

The closing seconds of the song (and album) feature Swift's voice, as if speaking to a private journal, saying, "I want to be defined by what

I love." Then *Lovers* fittingly ends with the final declaration, "You are what you love."

## Final Thoughts

Taylor Swift is somewhat of an enigma as a cultural icon. In a culture that continues to bang drums and declare that strong women "don't need no man," Swift's gospel continues to suggest that there is no peace or identity outside of a romantic relationship with a man. When I sat down to listen to *Lovers*, I braced myself for a barrage of politically charged anthems in line with the LGBT-driven first single, "You Need to Calm Down." There are a few of that type of song ("The Man" is a failed and highly ironic attempt at a feminist hymn and "Miss Americana & the Heartbreak Prince" is an anti-Republican political track). Overall, however, I was surprised by the lack of preachy tunes. Instead, *Lovers* offers something far more tragic and heartbreaking.

The album paints the portrait of a sad, lonely person who chases after peace in the arms of the false god of love only to find emptiness and hopelessness. Despite lyrics that rarely pierce beneath the surface (the lone exception being the incredibly moving song "Soon You'll Get Better" about her mother's cancer), Taylor Swift's lyrics manage to capture a snapshot of our generation that continues to travel ever further down an empty road in search of peace and spiritual satisfaction. *Lovers* ends with "Daylight," but we will have to wait until her next album is released in a few years to find out whether this light was true salvation or merely a fleeting glimpse of false hope through the clouds.

# 18

# Angry Birds 2 (Movie Review)

*An absolute abomination.*

## About the Film

Animated children's films have come a long way in recent years. Gone are the days when such films existed merely to bombard kids with spastic non-stop visuals and an endless parade of poop and fart jokes. Hollywood now understands that children are, in fact, intelligent beings capable of processing thoughtful themes and understanding clever humor. Well, *Angry Birds* 2 is a throw-back to former days . . . and not in a good way.

This film operates on the assumption that children are utterly stupid and then aims low. The "humor" is not just low-hanging fruit; it is fruit that has fallen off the tree and undergone weeks of decay and worm infestation. University research departments should be given sizable government grants to study and attempt to understand the unimaginable levels of idiocy this film manages to achieve. That this film is so wholly mindless would be more digestible if its makers had not gone a step further by cramming it full of mind-boggling sexual innuendos that have to be seen to be believed. The most scathing review I've ever written was for *Men in Black: International*, but *Angry Birds 2* makes that film look like *Citizen Kane*. I truly cannot recall a movie I have seen in the last few years—perhaps ever—that I detested more than this garbage heap.

## For Consideration

**On the Surface—(Profanity, Sexual Content, Violence, etc.).**

*Profanity:* At least three uses of "Oh my G—!" Also, although not technically classified as "profanities," parents should also be aware that this film is filled with other words like "crap," "stupid," "flipping," "butt," etc.

*Sexuality:* Oh boy. Buckle up and see comments below.

*Violence:* There is no gratuitous violence (ie. no blood and gore), but several birds and pigs straight-up die in horrible ways, such as getting crushed by rocks or consumed by lava. They might not actually *be* dead (I'm not sure if they appear in the background of later scenes), but in the scenes themselves they are goners.

**~~Beneath the Surface~~ Also on the Surface— (~~Themes, Philosophical Messages, Worldview, etc.~~)**

### 1. Sexuality and a Sick Perverted World

*Angry Birds 2* is the most sexually charged animated film I have ever been forced to endure. There are not one but *two* sexual innuendos that strongly suggest masturbation (!!!). The first is slightly less explicit. When Red (the protagonist bird) finds out that the pigs have been spying on his house with drones, he sheepishly asks, "Oh, so you've seen me...um..." to which the pig replies, "Yes, and it's disgusting." There is the possibility of a less vile interpretation of this moment, but a second scene later in the film removes any doubt that the film would "go there." In this scene, Bomb—the large black bird—is hiding behind a large lava lamp trying to hype himself up to attack the villainous eagles, unaware that he is clearly visible. The scene cuts to the eagles' perspective as they watch Bomb grunt and go through the shocking motions. The raised eyebrows and bewildered expressions on the eagles faces reveal what assumptions they are making.

It is difficult to fathom that a bunch of adult perverts were sitting around in a Hollywood studio boardroom and agreeing that what their film really needed more of was cartoon bird masturbation. Are there actually people out there amused by this type of "humor"? These two scenes are the worst offenses, but hardly the only ones. In another scene, the speedster yellow bird pranks the king pig by drawing a mustache on his face. When the pig turns around, we see that the bird has also drawn a "dog's face" on the pig's back—with the "eyes" clearly stand-ins for female breasts and the "tongue" for male genitals. There is a peeping-tom gag, multiple "guy wearing a thong" gags, and...well, you probably get the point.

## Final Verdict

This movie is utter trash. Did my 4-year-old boys catch or understand any of the many sexual innuendos? Thankfully, no. But leaving the theater of an animated kid's movie thinking, "Well, I hope my kids didn't catch all those sex and masturbation jokes" is not something any

101

parent should be forced to do. If *Angry Birds 2* doesn't end the year as the clear-cut worst movie of 2019, then I will renounce my faith in a benevolent and loving God. If you've been putting off any dental work or root canals, this film's 96-minute runtime would be far better off spent by taking care of that.

# 19

# Star Wars: The Rise of Skywalker (Movie Review)

*The Force is With Us Always, But It's Not As Strong As It Once Was.*

## About the Film

Star Wars is so much more than a series of goofy space films. For many people, it is an important part of our childhood and upbringing. The original three movies were the first non-cartoon films I ever saw as a kid (the day my father decided that it was time for boys to become men!). Now, as a father myself, the films are a special bond between me and my two 5-year-old twin boys. Beneath the surface of the lightsabers and dogfighting spacecrafts is Joseph Campbell's classic hero's journey and an almost therapeutic experience of childlike wonder. For this reason, reviewing a Star Wars film is difficult. *Jumanji* or *Frozen 2* didn't mean anything to me—Star Wars does.

I felt "much conflict" within me after I left the theater. To be honest, I felt a little let down and disappointed in the film. Thankfully, I decided to see it a second time before writing my review. In doing so, I was able to look past the trees and see the forest. Although there is much still to process about the film, I think that—despite several narrative flaws—the film is an emotionally satisfying end to the trilogy.

The movie asks *a lot* of viewers. Even the famous opening crawl introduces major game-changing plot points, and there are several huge developments that seemingly come out of left-field (and, given the behind-the-scenes drama and tug-o-war between directors Rian Johnson and JJ Abrams, they clearly *are* out of left field). The disconnect and lack of continuity between this film and *The Last Jedi*—the previous entry in the saga—is blatantly evident. Sometimes painfully so. Yet, if you are able to take the leap of faith and accept the film without getting bogged down in narrative details or too many questions, there is a lot to appreciate and enjoy here. Characters repeatedly say throughout the movie that the Force is an almost indescribable *feeling*. The same might be said of Star Wars as a whole. The saga has never been overly complicated, intellectual, or even logical—but, when done right, the films capture a certain Star Wars "feeling." *The Rise of Skywalker* is far from a cinematic masterpiece, but it *felt* like Star Wars, and at least for me, that's enough.

## For Consideration

**On the Surface—(Profanity, Sexual content, Violence, etc.)**

*Profanity:* A few minor profanities (A—, D—, H—)

*Sexuality:* The much publicized first LGBTQ moment in Star Wars is a background kiss between two celebrating women. It's a "blink-and-you-miss-it" moment, but also a likely—and unfortunate—sign of things to come for the series going forward.

*Violence:* I found this installment more violent than a typical Star Wars film. One moment in which a villain melts (a la *Indiana Jones and the Raiders of the Lost Ark)* is particularly gruesome.

## Beneath the Surface— (Themes, Philosophical Messages, Worldview, etc.)

### 1. The Choice Between Light Side and Dark Side

Star Wars has always been a balance between Science-Fiction and Fantasy. Whereas *The Last Jedi* leaned into the Sci-Fi elements, *The Rise of Skywalker* returns to the more fantastical side. The Force is front and center. While the previous film explored concepts such as the gray area between light/dark and good/evil, this film returns to the simpler duality that good is good, bad is bad, and we must make our choice between the two. That is not to say that characters are without flaws, only that *Rise of Skywalker* affirms that these flaws are not the end of the story. At one point, a character declares that the Dark Side is in the person's very nature. Later, the film triumphantly declares that we are not bound to where we came from or our flawed nature. We have a choice. While some Christians have historically found the mysticism of the Force problematic, I believe when taken on a more thematic level, this hopeful message is welcome, uplifting, and powerful.

### 2. Restoration and Redemption

Restoration and redemption have always been at the heart of Star Wars. In *Rise of Skywalker,* these themes are evident on both an individual level and also on a larger generational level. In *The Last Jedi,* Rian Johnson toyed with the theme that the previous generations were imperfect and left their big mess of failures and baggage as a burden for the younger generations to carry and attempt to clean up. *Rise of Skywalker* turns this idea on its head. A common theme woven throughout the story is that the older generations must restore and elevate the younger generations, empowering and blessing them to fight their own fight. During a climatic final pep-talk, Poe declares that the good guys need to confront the evil of their time just as their parents did in their own day. In this way, the film (and the new trilogy as a whole) is able to celebrate—rather than negate—the achievements of Luke, Leia, Han, and the original band of heroes. Whereas *Last Jedi* had a distinctly cynical and almost nihilistic edge to it, *Rise of Skywalker* is unabashedly optimistic and hopeful. I, for one, am thankful for this shift.

## Final Verdict

Much like Luke Skywalker's pivotal test in the Dark Side Cave on Dagobah, I think many viewers will find in this movie "only what they bring with them." People looking for a crisply scripted masterpiece that rekindles all the same feelings and emotions as the original films will undoubtably be disappointed. Viewers hoping for the film to go into bold and uncharted territory—as *The Last Jedi* did—will likely be let down as well. But if you go into the film without strong expectations and are able to surrender yourself to the ride, this movie is a fitting and satisfying end to a trilogy that I think ultimately didn't fully live up to its promised potential. The Force may not be as strong as it once was when a budding filmmaker named George Lucas was making a goofy space flick in the 1970s, but *Rise of Skywalker* is nevertheless a reminder that the Force is still with us—*always.*

# 20

# Little Women (2019) (Movie Review)

Written by Carrie Blackaby Camp

*A refreshing adaptation of a timeless story.*

### About the Film

A predominantly female cast of strong characters who resist society's narrow expectations for them and know how to handle themselves in traditionally male arenas.

Nope, I'm not referring to *Ghostbusters* (2016), *Ocean's 8* (2018), or *Captain Marvel* (2019). I'm talking about a classic story that has been a staple of American literature for 150 years.

In case you missed the book and the previous three dozen adaptations, *Little Women* follows Jo March, an aspiring writer, her three sisters, and her mother as they live in a romantic state of poverty while their father is away serving as a chaplain in the Civil War. (Somehow, despite their constant complaints about being poor, they can still afford a housekeeper, plenty of food, and a tidy little home. Oh, to be so poor!)

As a purist who read the book multiple times during high school and has fond memories of watching earlier film adaptations (usually around Christmas), I was skeptical that this iteration would live up to my high standards. Because, let's face it, *Little Women* is not something we want to see tarnished by a shoddy remake.

But I was surprisingly pleased with director Greta Gerwig's adaptation. Not only does it capture the whimsical charm of the book, but it is also beautifully filmed and tweaked to make the story fresh and relevant for a new generation. If anything, the changes Gerwig made to the original, predominantly relating to chronology, actually *strengthened* the story.

I can imagine this film becoming a staple for the next generation of *Little Women* fans.

## For Consideration
### On the Surface—(Profanity, Sexual Content, Violence, etc.).

*Profanity:* None.

*Sexuality:* There are some brief kisses.

*Violence:* None, though a few accidents and serious illnesses are depicted (but in a tame, non-gory way).

## Beneath the Surface— (Themes, Philosophical Messages, Worldview, etc.)

1.**Feminism, feminism, and more feminism.** *Little Women* was a feminist story long before the advent of all-female remakes, social justice warriors, and "girl power" twitter hashtags. Louisa May Alcott (author of *Little Women*) was a woman ahead of her times. So, it's not shocking that feminist themes are central to the film and often peppered generously into the dialogue. Set during and shortly after the Civil War, Jo March defies the strict gender stereotypes of her day, most notably by pursuing a career as a writer (a field that was largely closed to women at the time) and by frequently voicing her opinion of marriage as something that boxes women in and takes away their freedom. Amy, the youngest March sister, also gives a passionate speech about marriage being a decision driven by economy rather than feeling. And even the dour Aunt March talks plainly about the daughters marrying well (aka, *rich*) being the family's only hope. All of that was to be expected.

What *did* surprise me was the film's refreshingly balanced take on feminism. Rather than the brash, man-hating, #SmashThePatriarchy fourth-wave feminism that has recently dominated the media, *Little Women* took a much more tempered approach. It managed to tackle gender injustices—such as the few career paths open to women at the time—without denigrating the value of marriage and family. In one of the most moving and honest scenes, Jo, an unabashed feminist, admits that while she abhors the idea of being trapped in a loveless marriage, she is actually *really lonely*. By admitting that she may *not* feel entirely fulfilled as an independent career woman, Jo questions some of the tenets of today's feminist ideology.

Another memorable line comes from Meg, who gently admonishes Jo for criticizing her decision to marry, saying, "Just because my dreams are different than yours doesn't make them less important." Her words give a much-needed voice to women in today's "woke" culture who find fulfilment in more traditional gender roles, a demographic that is often marginalized by more militant feminists.

2. **The nobility of sacrifice and a struggle for personal virtue.** Another theme in the movie is the importance of self-sacrifice and living a virtuous life, even when doing so is uncomfortable. The March family's sacrifices range from enormous (living without their husband/father while he serves their country) to small (giving their own Christmas breakfast to a family in need). The characters also talk a lot about being "good" and their desire to become more virtuous, something Marmee—the saint-like mother—instills in her daughters. Though, with the exception of Beth, they never achieve that perfect standard, their desire for personal betterment is a worthy goal they constantly strive for.

## Final Verdict

Gerwig's adaptation of *Little Women* is heartwarming, funny, and enjoyable for long-time fans and newbies alike with strong performances from the core cast. Though the use of flashbacks is somewhat confusing at times, they largely strengthen the story and add some interesting parallelism that is missing in the original version. Overall, it is one of the better remakes of recent years.

# Notes

1. Donald Goddard, "From 'American Graffiti' to Outer Space." in *The New York Times*. September 12, 1976, 86.

2. Neal Gabler. *An Empire of Their Own.* (New York: Anchor Books, 1989), 119.

3. Plato. *Republic: Barnes & Nobel Classics Series.* trans. Benhamin Jowett (New York: Barnes & Nobel Books, 2004), 334.

4. Patrick Markey, cited in Mae Anderson, "No, there's still no link between video games and violence." *APnews.com.* August 6, 2019. Accessed January 13, 2020.

5. C. S. Lewis. "On Three Ways of Writing for Children" in *On Stories: And Essays on Literature* (Washington, PA: Harvest Books, 2002), 40.

6. See https://www.pewforum.org/2018/04/25/when-americans-say-they-believe-in-god-what-do-they-mean/

7. Thomas Nagel. *The Last Word* (New York: Oxford University Press, 2001), 130.

8. See https://www.barna.com/research/meet-love-jesus-not-church/

# Dr. Daniel Blackaby

Daniel started The Collision in 2019 because of his passion for pop culture and the creative arts and his desire to encourage other Christians to join the cultural conversations happening around them. He holds a PhD in Christianity and the Arts and a ThM in Philosophy, Worldview, and Apologetics from The Southern Baptist Theological Seminary. He is the author/co-author of multiple fiction and nonfiction books, including *When Worlds Collide: Stepping Out and Standing Out in an Anti-God Culture* and the YA Fantasy trilogy *The Lost City Chronicles*. He lives in Jonesboro, Georgia, with his wife Sarah and twin boys, Emerson and Logan.

**Twitter:** @danielblackaby
**Facebook:** @danielblackabyauthor

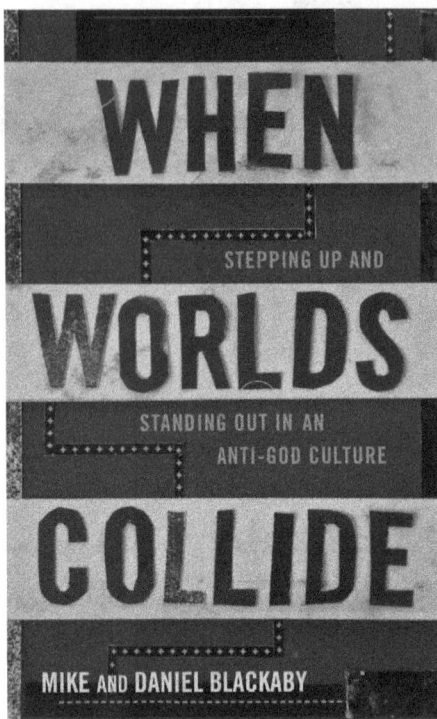

# WHEN WORLDS COLLIDE

*by Mike & Daniel Blackaby*

The media-driven world places enormous pressure on people to conform to its secular point of view. *When Worlds Collide* is the Blackabys' case for becoming a Collider— Christians who remain true to their faith while effectively engaging the world and being used by God to change people's lives.

In chapters packed with story-based devotional thoughts, plenty of humor, and easy steps for application, they prove it's possible to live an authentic Christian life that meets the world head-on without spiritual compromise.

THE COLLISION
EXPERIENCING GOD IN TODAY'S CULTURE

The Collision is a digital, multi-media platform aimed at equipping Christians to navigate the inevitable collisions between Christ and culture. At the Collision, you can find thought-provoking articles on contemporary cultural topics, reviews of all the latest Hollywood movies written from a Christian perspective, and a community of Christians committed to engaging the world for Christ.

*Join the movement today:*

**Website:** thecollision.org
**YouTube:** youtube.com/c/thecollisionbmi
**Facebook:** @TheCollisionbmi
**Twitter:** @TheCollisionbmi

www.ingramcontent.com/pod-product-compliance
Lightning Source LLC
Chambersburg PA
CBHW060114050426
42448CB00010B/1861